Inspiring | Educating | Creating | Entertaining

Brimming with creative inspiration, how-to projects, and useful information to enrich your everyday life, quarto.com is a favorite destination for those pursuing their interests and passions.

First published in 2022 by Rock Point, an imprint of The Quarto Group,
142 West 36th Street, 4th Floor, New York, NY 10018, USA
T (212) 779-4972 F (212) 779-6058 www.Quarto.com

Rock Point titles are also available at discount for retail, wholesale, promotional, and bulk purchase. For details, contact the Special Sales Manager by email at specialsales@quarto.com or by mail at The Quarto Group, Attn: Special Sales Manager, 100 Cummings Center Suite 265D, Beverly, MA 01915 USA.

10 9 8 7 6 5 4 3 2 1

ISBN: 978-1-63106-815-7

Publisher: Rage Kindelsperger
Creative Director: Laura Drew
Managing Editor: Cara Donaldson
Editor: Keyla Pizarro-Hernández
Cover and Interior Design: Amy Sly

This journal provides general information on various widely known and widely accepted topics that tend to evoke feelings of strength and confidence. However, it should not be relied upon as recommending or promoting any specific diagnosis or method of treatment for a particular condition, and it is not intended as a substitute for medical advice or for direct diagnosis and treatment of a medical condition by a qualified physician. Readers who have questions about a particular condition, possible treatments for that condition, or possible reactions from the condition or its treatment should consult a physician or other qualified healthcare professional.

Printed in China

May this journal soothe, calm, and heal.

May it spread love.

May it help connect us to our higher selves.

table of contents

1

Meet Your Anxiety

2

Anxiety as a Friend

3

Mindfulness

4

Thoughts

5

Emotions

6

Body

7

8

Experience

Forward from Here

HOW TO USE THIS JOURNAL

Hello and welcome, beautiful friend!

I am so glad you are here with me.

If your anxiety has taken over your life a little—or a lot—then you are in the right place. In this journal, we are going to move together toward a place where you can find more calm—where you can feel more informed, empowered, and ready to more easily meet the reality of your life.

Trust yourself. Go at your own pace. The practices in this book build on one another, from chapter to chapter, so it's best to do them in order. Any of the practices can be repeated as many times as you like—feel free to simply repeat them in a blank journal or on loose paper.

Many people are surprised to hear that, as a meditation instructor and spiritual teacher, I deal with anxiety on a personal level. After a decade plus of meditating and following a Buddhist path, going on tons of retreats, and receiving training and spiritual transmissions in a wide variety of healing modalities, I have learned a universal truth: life is effing stressful.

I'll bet you already figured out that little nugget of wisdom on your own. Because the truth is, we can do all the #selfcare in the world, download every meditation app in existence, and paper our walls with positive affirmations, and we'll still live in a world of increasingly volatile global economic, environmental, and systemic problems. So, if you are suffering from increasing or even debilitating anxiety, know this: you are not alone. Anxiety is both normal and common. A third of us are diagnosed with an anxiety disorder at some point in our lives, and I am going to venture a guess that a lot more of us suffer from anxiety these days.

Experiencing anxiety in this world means that you are a kind and gentle human whose soul is reacting in a wholly appropriate way to the chaos and actually impossible expectations of the world we live in today. But—and here's the good news—you don't have to live under the shadow of anxiety. Life is absolutely stressful. But there is a gentler, kinder, less anxious way to be in this world, and this journal will help you get there.

Everything in this journal may not work for you (everyone's experiences, anxiety triggers, and bodies are different), but I promise that if you do this work, you will find information and practices in here that will help change your life.

Whether you've had a formal diagnosis of some kind of anxiety disorder or not, if you experience anxiety, this book is for you. It is not crucial to have a diagnosis, or to know which "formal category" of anxiety you are currently experiencing, in order to do the work successfully.

As we will learn, anxiety does not technically get "cured." But we can learn to work with it, prevent it, reduce the symptoms, heal any underlying trauma, change our thinking, stop the spiral, and find more calm.

The path to ease our suffering from anxiety has eight steps. These are: meeting and understanding what anxiety really is; understanding how it can be a friend to us; learning to use mindfulness practices; using our thoughts to support us (instead of driving us mad); turning strong emotions into allies; connecting to the wisdom in our bodies; testing out all of this in the laboratory of our own life; and developing a practical plan for moving forward. We'll do all of this safely—you will be in charge of your own experiences here.

The practices in this journal are based on the principles of cognitive behavioral therapy, acceptance and commitment therapy, mindfulness, and somatic awareness. This journal is designed to stand on its own, but it also works well in conjunction with therapy and other mental health treatments. I encourage you to get as much help and support as you can.

A note for those living with disabilities: while some of the instructions might not suit your abilities or lived reality precisely, please feel confident that any modifications you might make in order to be more comfortable are welcome here. The most important thing is to be gentle and loving with yourself.

The information and exercises in this journal do not constitute medical advice. I am not a doctor. Always seek the guidance of a doctor or a mental health professional with questions you have about your own health and well-being.

There is a path out of the anxiety cycle! You have already taken the biggest step by being open to this work. I see you, and I am so grateful to be here with you.

May we be blessed and protected as we walk this path together.

Let's get started.

Liza

1) meet & understand what anxiety is

2) understand how it can be a friend

3) learn mindfulness practices

4) use our thoughts to support us

5) turn strong emotions into allies

6) connect w/ the wisdom in our bodies

7) test this in the "lab of life"

8) develop a practical plan to move forward.

P.S. THERE ARE FREE GUIDED VERSIONS OF ALL OF THE MEDITATIONS IN THIS JOURNAL AVAILABLE TO YOU AT LIZAKINDRED.COM/ANXIETY-JOURNAL-EXTRAS.

I LEARNED
MY ANXIETY,
AND I WILL
UNLEARN IT.

meet your anxiety

At its core, anxiety is a fear that we learned through experience. It can help to think of anxiety like a stress that has spread—either spread out from the original stressor to include other worries or spread out over time to focus on the past or future.

The symptoms of anxiety happen in the present moment, but the focus of anxiety is a fear about what could go wrong. Anxiety is based on things that have happened to us—and the fact that it is based on *real* experiences is important to know.

Anxiety is one of those things that can be tricky to explain to someone, but we know when we are having it. It can manifest as an energy (like feeing wired), as thought patterns (worrying ourselves into a tizzy), as emotions (feeling angry), or as physical symptoms (feeling sick to our stomach). Often, anxiety manifests as a combination of many or all of these components.

Anxiety often causes us to avoid: people, places, and things. This makes sense in the short term, but in the long term, avoidance reinforces anxiety and can make it worse.

Both anxiety and the methods for calming anxiety are informed by our "cognitive schemas"—our frameworks for understanding the world. As humans, we learn superfast. So, if we live through danger or uncertainty, our brains become attuned to danger and uncertainty. We develop what is called "attentional bias to threat," which means that bad stuff happened to us, so we watch out for more bad stuff.

This isn't "being negative." This is a biological survival mechanism. It is actually quite necessary to the survival of our human species. Being attuned to danger and threats is not a bad thing; it's a good thing. It's just that (like all good things) too much can become harmful.

Take water intake, for instance: I used to think that I should drink as much water as I possibly could, until I developed pernicious anemia from flooding my body with water and eventually I couldn't process vitamin B_{12}. I had no idea this could happen. That experience doesn't mean that drinking water is bad for me—it's still good. But I had to learn to moderate and regulate my water intake. Working with our anxiety is the process of moderating and regulating a good thing, too.

It's crucial to know and to understand that we learn anxiety. I don't mean that we learn how to be anxious (that comes naturally, ha!), but that we become anxious about things because things have happened that have given us reasons to feel anxious. You didn't make this stuff up.

Anxiety is based in reality. But, crucially, it is not our current reality.

Anxiety spreads out—it spirals and extrapolates and imagines and remembers and predicts and catastrophizes and makes big leaps. But part of why anxiety can be so tricky to work with is that it does start with something real. Maybe you had a stressful or even traumatizing experience. Perhaps you saw or heard of something happening to someone else. Or maybe you are imagining what could go wrong. Regardless of what happened that triggered our anxiety, it started with real and often valid fears. By knowing this, we can begin to meet our anxiety as a kind of truth-teller of sorts (albeit one that's become a little confused).

Often we can pretty quickly get to the root of an anxious moment, but it's not always that simple or straightforward; X does not always equal Y. And that's why sometimes anxiety can be confusing and you might think to yourself: "Why do I feel like this?" or "What is wrong with me?" (Spoiler alert: nothing.)

But the good news is, it isn't necessary to find the initial cause in order to calm the anxiety, and anxiety doesn't need to "make sense."

This is because learning a fear happens at a body ("somatic") and subconscious ("precognitive neurological") level. This is full-on survival mode stuff—it is our lizard brain keeping us safe. This is why we can't "convince" ourselves to "just let it go" or tell ourselves, "It's okay, you are safe and everything is fine," and then just . . . be calm. It doesn't work that way. (I suspect you already know this.)

While talking ourselves out of anxious feelings doesn't work, there are things that do work to calm anxiety, which is what we will do together here.

Anxiety breeds more anxiety, and we can often feel like we are stuck in a loop. When we become stressed out, we get jumpy and hyperaroused, so we start to notice all of the potential danger signs.

In other words: what makes us anxious? Having anxiety!

This can feel maddening. We can get ourselves out of that loop, though, and the work you do in this journal will help teach you exactly what works for you. And the same way that anxiety breeds more anxiety, calm breeds more calm! It doesn't take much to begin to step out of the cycle, as we'll learn; it just has to be the right steps for you.

Let's dive in!

Reflection

Before we dive into the work of understanding our anxiety a little bit better, let's take a moment to check in. Notice your body, emotions, energy, surroundings, and thoughts. How are you feeling, right now?

1/17 therapy w/ Dwight: you can have smarts and still miss things. Balance... take time to recognize things about myself.

Humor - look into keeping it alive important

How are you feeling about the idea of working with your anxiety?

....
....
....
....
....
....
....
....
....
....
....
....
....
....
....
....
....
....
....
....
....
....

BEFORE YOU GO ANY FURTHER, CLOSE OR REST YOUR EYES AND TAKE A MOMENT TO ACKNOWLEDGE HOW BRAVE YOU ARE TO DO THIS WORK.

The Anxiety Monster

Let's indulge in a bit of silliness. If anxiety were a monster, what do you think it might look like? Draw it here. It can be as mean or silly as it feels.

What are some things that your anxiety monster likes to say? Do your best to fill all of the bubbles; when you feel like you've filled out as many as you can, cross off the bubbles with a giant X.

Categorizing

Looking back at the things that anxiety monster likes to say, you will likely notice some common threads that run through them. Categories might be things like "reasons I might not be good enough" or "specific things that could go wrong."

What categories of messages does your anxiety send? Name and explain them.

....

....

....

....

....

....

....

....

....

....

....

....

....

....

....

....

....

....

....

Mindful Pause

What small thing can you do for yourself right now, in this moment, to care for yourself? Write it down here, and then go do it!

Biggest Worry Buttons

Anxiety often spins up negative core beliefs about ourselves because these beliefs tend to be our biggest worries—not because these things are true, but because we don't want them to be. These are our "core belief buttons," which could also be called our "biggest worry buttons." (Go gently and slowly in this exercise.)

Looking back at the categories of messages that your anxiety sends you, what "biggest worry buttons" is it trying to push?

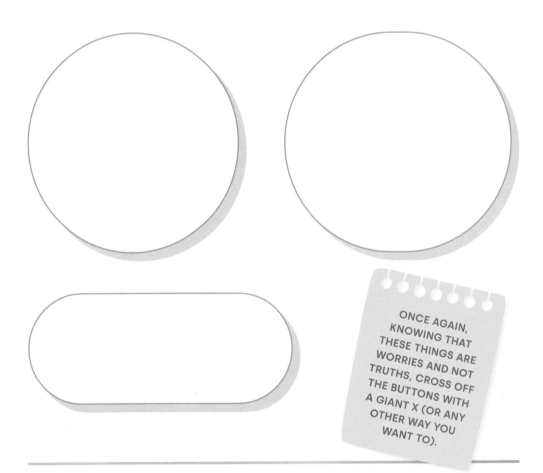

ONCE AGAIN, KNOWING THAT THESE THINGS ARE WORRIES AND NOT TRUTHS, CROSS OFF THE BUTTONS WITH A GIANT X (OR ANY OTHER WAY YOU WANT TO).

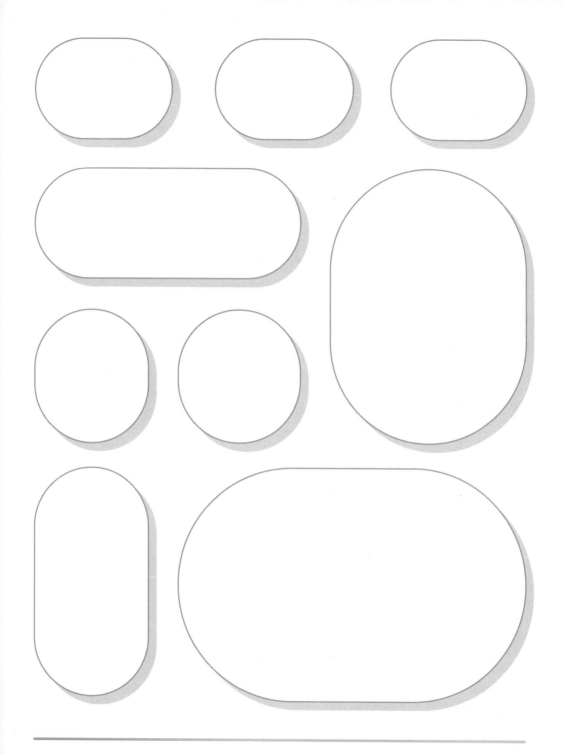

Examining My Anxiety

Every single person experiences anxiety differently, based on culture, community, body, and life experiences. Circle the words that stand out for you as being descriptive of or relevant to your personal anxiety. Let your eyes wander over the page, knowing that these words are representations, not suggestions. This is not a checklist!

Argumentative

Dread or doom

Avoidance   Dry mouth

Blank mind

Embarrassment

Camouflaging   Evade

Chest pain

Fatigue

Chills   Floating

Clenched teeth

Freeze

Clinging   Head feels hot

Clumsy

Head rush

Compulsion   Headache

Confusion

Hiding

Digestion issues   Hot flashes

Diminished

Impulsive

Discursive thinking   Insomnia

Disgusted

Intolerant

Dizziness   Itching

Mind playing tricks   Rituals

            Mind racing   Sensory overload

Monkey mind   Shortness of breath

            Muscle tension   Skin picking

Nausea   Something is "off"

            Nerve pain   Squeezing

Nervousness   Stomach churning

            Obsession   Stomach pain

Panic   Tight jaw

            Paranoia   Tightness in throat

Phobic   Tingling

            Pickiness   Tongue biting

Pins and needles   Twitching

            Preoccupied   Uncertain

Quiet   Unease

            Racing heart   Unfocused

Rashes   Ungrounded

            Restlessness   Weak heart

Rising heat   Wind blowing through

After looking at the words you circled, on a separate piece of
paper, write down what stands out to you about your experience
of anxiety. Some people notice their culture, community, or family
values in their anxiety symptoms. Do you notice anything like that?
What else stands out?

My Best Strategies So Far

You are the biggest expert on your own anxiety. What steps, strategies, practices, or self-care moves are generally pretty good at helping you calm your anxiety? These might not be things that always work, but they do sometimes.

....

....

....

....

....

....

....

....

....

....

....

....

....

....

....

....

....

....

....

....

Gratitude Moment

Before we close out this chapter, let's do a quick practice:

Place one or both hands over your heart. Close or rest your eyes. Notice any energy, emotions, or warmth that you might feel. Take ten slow, deep breaths, focusing on a long exhale. When you are done, place your hands gently in your lap, open your eyes, and smile.

Now, look back at the work you did in this section to understand more about your anxiety. How are you feeling right now, in this very moment? What are you grateful for?

PUT YOUR ANXIETY DOWN; WE ARE FINISHED EXAMINING IT. EXHALE DEEPLY.

YOU CAN'T
HATE
YOURSELF
INTO
SOMEONE YOU
CAN LOVE.

CHAPTER 2

CALM YOUR ANXIETY JOURNAL

anxiety as a friend

When we fight against our anxiety, it gets worse. Whatever we've tried, it's probably very clear to us that hoping and wishing anxiety away doesn't work. What does work, though, is learning to make friends with our anxiety and working *with* it, instead of against it.

It might seem a little "out there" at first, the idea of making friends with our anxiety—the thing that interrupts our life and so often seems to make everything more difficult for us than it needs to be. But if you can stick with the work of this chapter, I believe that you will start to understand—deeply understand—why and how our anxiety can be our ally, and why working with it is so much more effective than working against it.

By respecting and honoring our anxiety, by treating it with compassion, by meeting it with curiosity, and by seeing the reasons to be grateful for it, we can turn a former foe into a fantastic friend that only shows up for us when we really need it. It matters a lot to be able to understand the origins, characteristics, and good intentions of anxiety because that is how we can work with it—and even be friendly with it.

Anxiety develops when our protection instincts (good things to have; they take care of us) get a little hypervigilant . . . or maybe a lot hypervigilant. Anxiety stems from self-protection mechanisms and from being attuned to threats (both real and perceived) so that we can get the information we need to take care of ourselves and keep ourselves safe.

At its core, our anxiety is saying to us: "Hold up, friend! I sense some potential for danger here, and I want to keep you safe." To which we are going to learn to say: "Thank you, anxiety. I appreciate that. I hear you, and I can take it from here. You can go now."

We can respect, honor, and work with our anxiety when we are able to recognize the ways it can and will be helpful to us.

What happens to those healthy self-protection mechanisms is that anxiety is like, "Cool, I really want to help. If a little vigilance or reminding you of past troubles is helpful, I am going to do a lot of that for you, because I care *so much*." It's like someone you know who is really meaning to be supportive, and is trying really hard, but they are just not helpful.

You've probably tried different anxiety coping mechanisms (such as avoiding things that make you anxious) and likely found some short-term relief from them. That is well and good, but these won't work as *long-term* solutions, because they are still *inside* the anxiety cycle— still stuck in that loop. But you're going to learn some long-term ways to work with anxiety to reduce it over time instead of reinforcing it. Ultimately, you will learn to calm your anxiety in a way that helps you in the moment *and* over the long term.

I am what I like to think of as a very good party host. But once I had a friend helping me prepare for a party, and I was running down a list of things that could go wrong, like: we need more ice in case we run out; do we have anything for someone who is vegan and gluten free; let's make sure no one gets burnt by a lit candle; and so on. She got annoyed with me and said, "Stop worrying so much! Your parties are always great. It will be fine."

I immediately felt defensive. But using mindfulness and self-reflection I became curious about my strong reaction. I realized my parties are great *because* I worry so much. I always think through what could go wrong, and I plan or prepare for it. My anxiety has paradoxically helped me become a better party host.

If you do start feeling heated or defensive or have an urge to stand up for your worrying or anxiety-based behaviors, that's cool and very welcome here! Because that means that you already, on some level, respect and appreciate what anxiety can do for you.

So to be very clear: we're not talking smack and we're not hating on our personalities—you are perfect just the way you are. We're just putting *you* lovingly at the helm. We can relearn how to relate to the anxiety loop while being thankful and respectful of why we developed it in the first place.

At the same time, we are not protecting or amplifying our anxiety; our ultimate goal is to reduce it, so that it only shows up when it is needed and helpful. And one of the ways we can do that is by listening to it, so that it doesn't get extra on us.

So, let's make a new friend together.

Hello, anxiety.
I am listening.

For this practice, we are going to give our anxiety our full attention as a way to understand what it wants us to know. Find a comfortable, quiet place where you feel safe. Take a few deep, slow breaths. Place your hands over your heart, close or rest your eyes, and say with a soft voice, "Hello, anxiety. I am here, and I am listening. I welcome you to tell me what it is you want me to hear." And then . . . listen. Pay attention to what comes up—it could be emotions, physical sensations, thoughts, energies, or impulses.

What do you hear?

....
....
....
....
....
....
....
....
....
....
....

continues ↪

My Anxiety as Signposts

All of our emotions, including anxiety, can act as helpful signposts for us. When we enter into a dialogue with our anxiety, we are entering into conversation with our deepest selves. Find a comfortable, quiet place where you feel safe. Take a few deep, slow breaths. Place your hands over your heart, close or rest your eyes, and say with a soft voice, "Hello, anxiety. I am here, and I am listening. What signals do you have for me about my . . . ?"

What signals do you have for me about my environment? *(Examples: overstimulating, smells good, feels safe or unsafe)*

....
....
....
....
....

What signals do you have for me about my body? *(Examples: thirsty, craves more movement)*

....
....
....
....

What signals do you have for me about my relationships? *(Examples: how certain people make me feel, boundaries to set)*

....
....
....
....
....
....
....
....

What signals do you have for me about the other parts of my life?

....
....
....
....
....
....
....

CLOSE THE PRACTICE BY PLACING YOUR HANDS OVER YOUR HEART AND SAYING, "THANK YOU, ANXIETY. I HEARD YOU. YOU MAY GO."

Anxiety into Action

One of the neat things that anxiety can do is spur us into necessary action. Not always—sometimes it can paralyze us into inaction—but for this exercise, let's look at some of the ways anxiety or worrying has helped us do things that we are glad we did.

How has your anxiety turned worries into action?

ANXIETY	ACTION
I worry about my financial future.	*I started a savings account.*
→	
→	
→	
→	
→	

ANXIETY	ACTION
	→
	→
	→
	→
	→
	→
	→
	→

CLOSE WITH GRATITUDE.

Mindful Pause

How are you feeling so far about taking a closer look at your anxiety? What have you noticed coming up?

How Has My Anxiety Helped Me?

Think again about the ways anxiety has protected, guided, or served you. In what broad ways has your anxiety helped you over your life? Kept you safe? Looked out for you? Encouraged you to do what was needed?

....

....

....

....

....

....

....

....

....

....

....

....

....

....

....

....

FINISH WITH A MOMENT OF GRATITUDE FOR YOUR ANXIETY AND ALL THAT IT HAS DONE FOR YOU.

Greetings, Anxiety

When our anxiety starts spinning out, we tend to greet it without much kindness, but let's consider some other ways we could possibly acknowledge or greet our anxiety.

When I start to feel anxiety, I often think:

....

....

....

....

....

....

....

Some other ways I could greet my anxiety:

Examples to get you started:

☐ *Welcome, darling. What do you need today?*

☐ *Hello. I see you. What message do you want me to hear?*

☐ *Hi, I see you, my sweet thing, but I am busy today. How important is this?*

☐ ....

☐ ....

Mark one or more to try.

FINISH WITH YOUR HANDS OVER YOU HEART, LETTING YOUR ANXIETY KNOW THAT YOU WILL OCCASIONALLY GREET IT WITH A BIT MORE KINDNESS AND WARMTH.

A Love Letter to Anxiety

Dear Anxiety,

It's been a long road! Here are some things I would like you to know: ....

....

....

....

....

....

....

....

....

....

....

....

....

....

....

....

....

....

How Can I Help My Anxiety?

Now that you know your anxiety and what it is trying to tell you a little bit better, let's look at specific ways you can be helpful to your anxiety.

How can I be helpful to my anxiety?

....

....

....

....

....

....

....

In what ways might I help my anxiety help me?

....

....

....

....

....

....

....

FINISH WITH HANDS ON YOUR HEART, LETTING YOUR ANXIETY KNOW THAT YOU ARE LOOKING FORWARD TO A HEALTHIER RELATIONSHIP WITH IT.

Gratitude

Look back at the work you did in this section about making friends with your anxiety. Take a moment to notice what you are grateful for and write it down here.

PRESENT
MOMENT
AWARENESS
IS A
SUPERPOWER.

mindfulness

What is mindfulness?

Mindfulness is, simply, nonjudgmental awareness. It's the state of being connected to and aware of the present moment—without judging it. It offers us a powerful way to relate to our thoughts, as well as to our bodies, emotions, and the world around us.

Once we have established an awareness of our thoughts and thought patterns, we begin to change how we relate to them and can start to work with them. Using mindfulness, we step into the observer role instead of identifying as our thoughts.

Leaving the present moment—slipping into memories of the past or fears about the future—is how anxiety gets its purchase. Connecting to the present moment through mindful awareness helps take us out of the cycle of focusing on what could go wrong and into the reality of what is. It's a way of developing trust in our experience.

Both the present moment awareness and the nonjudgmental parts of mindfulness matter, but it can be especially tricky to not judge ourselves when we are caught in anxiety. Here's an example:

Noticing the sharp feeling of cold wind on our skin, we can observe: "I'm cold." This is us being aware of what's happening in the moment. But when we move into "I'm cold and I hate being cold," then we are moving into judgment and are no longer anchored in the present moment. At this point we are identifying with the judgment instead of having a direct experience of the cold. And judging what's happening as "bad" or undesirable in some way exacerbates the negative impact; we move from having an experience to having a bad experience.

Listen—some stuff just sucks. I will never tell you to "just stay positive." Part of present moment awareness is noticing all of reality—the good, the bad, and the sucky. We're showing up for all of what is. But on an everyday level, studies show that we are happier even while doing things we dislike if we can stay fully present for them. Surprise, right?

Try mindfulness the next time you're doing something you dislike—maybe the dishes. Really notice the feeling of warm water, the glints of light on the silverware, the casual symphony of the rattling dishes. You may not become a huge fan of doing dishes, but it is possible to use mindfulness to enjoy the process a little bit.

The words *mindfulness* and *meditation* are sometimes used interchangeably, but they are actually two different yet related things. Mindfulness, as we covered, is a quality or state of being—being present in the moment. Meditation, on the other hand, is the practice of intentionally directing our attention to something—meditating on it.

The most common type of meditation in the West is, in fact, mindfulness meditation. In this practice, we use an anchor (often the breath) to bring our attention to the present moment. As our mind wanders (which it will!), we simply notice that—become mindful of it—and bring our attention back to our present moment anchor, again and again. This is mindfulness meditation.

While meditation and mindfulness are having a "moment" right now, the basic teachings and practices are based on principles that are thousands of years old. You can rest assured that this stuff really works.

Letting all manner of things be as they are—adopting an attitude of acceptance about them—actually decreases symptoms of anxiety. Practicing this with our thoughts diffuses their power and reduces their ability to control us. We're not actually trying to control our thoughts or eliminate them. (This shouldn't be the aim of meditation and doesn't work anyway.)

But what mindfulness does allow us to do is find a healthy, empowering way to disconnect from the stories that can spiral out of control, and to anchor ourselves in the present moment—so that we can meet what is actually happening instead of being overtaken by anxiety.

Modifications for Meditations

Always feel free to modify the instructions in this book to help you feel as safe and comfortable as possible. If closing your eyes causes stress, gently rest them instead. Let them soften; take in the colors and shapes. Release any tension around your eyes and gaze softly at the ground a few feet in front of you. Let things be a blurry haze, not taking anything in or keeping anything out. Just soften and rest your eyes. (And if it helps you to feel more safe, orient your body to face the door of the room you're in.)

If being extra-aware of your breath causes stress, focus on other physical sensations instead. Gently place your hands on your legs—not gripping, just resting. Focus on the sensations of your hands touching your body: the warmth, weight, texture, energy. Alternatively, focus on where your booty touches your seat, or your feet touch the floor. Here, also notice what's underneath you, rising up to meet and support you. If you start to feel ungrounded, use gentle self-touch to soothe and remind yourself that you are here for you.

You can feel confident in making the modifications that best support you.

Be Here Now

Get comfortable, take a long breath with a deep exhale, and look around you. DRAW what you see. (Don't worry about being accurate, or if you are drawing things near or far. This isn't about being an artist; it's about being an observer.)

Present Moment Awareness

Get comfortable, take a long breath with a deep exhale, and open your senses. What do you observe?

Colors:

....
....
....

Shapes:

....
....
....

Smells:

....
....
....

Temperature:

....
....
....

Sounds (near and far):

....

....

....

Textures or weight of things touching your body:

....

....

....

Lights:

....

....

....

What else?

....

....

....

....

....

....

....

YOU CAN USE THIS PRACTICE ANY TIME TO BECOME MORE CONNECTED TO THE PRESENT MOMENT. WHEN ANXIETY BEGINS TO RISE, LIST TO YOURSELF THREE THINGS YOU HEAR, THREE THINGS YOU SEE, AND THREE THINGS YOU FEEL.

Mindfulness Meditation

1. Find a relatively quiet, private space, and set a timer for 5 to 20 minutes (your choice).

2. Stretch out, then settle into a comfortable, upright posture.

3. Let your hands gently rest on your legs, in your lap, or in each other.

4. Gently rest or close your eyes.

5. Take a moment to check in with yourself: How do you feel emotionally? Physically? Energetically?

6. Take a few long, deep breaths, focusing on the exhale.

7. Bring your focused attention to the physical sensations of your breath, noticing where you feel it and what it feels like.

8. As your mind wanders, simply notice that, and bring your attention back to your breath.

9. Continue to gently refocus your attention until the time is up.

10. Take a final moment to check in with yourself once more. Has anything changed or shifted?

What did you notice during this meditation?

....
....
....
....
....
....
....
....
....
....
....
....
....
....
....
....
....
....
....
....

PLACE YOUR HAND OVER YOUR HEART AND GIVE YOURSELF A MOMENT OF GRATITUDE FOR THE PRACTICE.

Mindful Pause

Pick a regular, everyday activity to approach using mindful awareness. This could be something like brushing your teeth, getting dressed, cleaning off the counters—anything you'd be doing already. If it's something you normally go on "autopilot" for, that is a great choice. When your mind wanders from the present moment, just notice that and refocus your attention.

While you do this activity, notice:

+ The sounds of the activity.

+ The colors.

+ Any tastes or smells.

+ Textures, weights, or movements.

+ How do you engage your body with the activity?

+ Are you tempted to rush? To zone out?

What did you do?

....

....

....

....

....

What was it like? How did it feel? Did paying close attention to it change your experience in any way?

....

....

....

....

....

....

....

....

....

....

....

....

....

....

....

....

....

....

....

....

....

....

Object Meditation

Choose a small physical object to become the focus of a meditation—something small enough to hold easily in one hand. Pick something that you feel pretty neutral about. It can be anything, really—a pen, a coaster, a rock, a toy. Try not to overthink it. Aim for 5 to 10 minutes of full focus.

Get comfortable, take a slow breath (focusing on making the exhale long), and take a moment to check in with yourself. When you are ready, pick up the object in your hands, and notice:

+ What does the surface feel like?

+ What is the shape? Does it feel different or the same as it looks?

+ What colors do you see? Do they change as you move it in the light?

+ What weight does it have in your hands?

+ What temperature is it?

+ Does it have a smell?

+ What textures do you feel?

+ Does this object bring up any emotions?

+ What else do you notice?

When your mind wanders, just bring it back to the object. Take one last deep breath and set the object down, with gratitude.

What was this experience like? Did anything surprise you?

File Your Thoughts

Repeat the mindfulness meditation practice from page 54. This time, when you find your mind wandering, before you release the thought and return to focusing on your breath, you are going to notice what the thought is about—what category.

Every person and every meditation practice session is different, but you might notice categories like daydreaming or imagining, worries, guilt, things "to do" or "to remember," emotions, physical discomfort, distractions in the room, self-judgment, remembering funny or annoying things, and so on. It can run the gamut.

When you are finished, fill in the file folders below with the categories of thoughts you had. Be as specific as possible. When you are done, you will have learned a bit more about how your brain works.

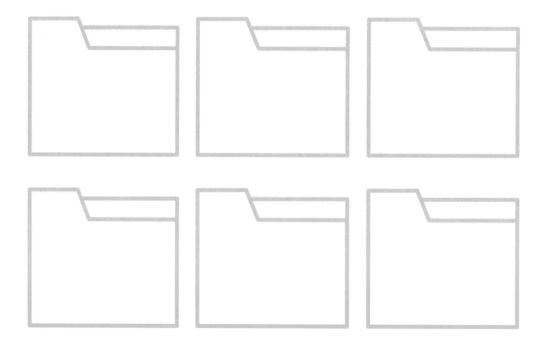

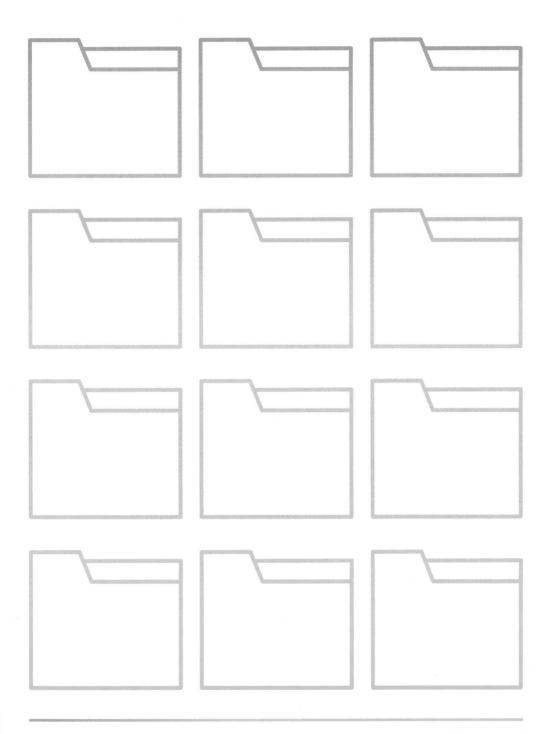

Morning Meditation

Many of us have different types of thinking patterns depending on whether we are at the start or end of our day. For this practice, first thing in the morning (even in bed, if you like!), repeat the mindfulness meditation practice from page 54. When you have finished, answer the following questions.

What was the experience like before the day started? What did you notice this morning?

....
....
....
....
....
....
....
....
....
....
....
....
....
....
....

Having done this practice to start your day, is there anything you'd like to remember to carry with you?

....
....
....
....
....
....
....
....
....
....
....
....
....
....
....
....
....
....

Evening Meditation

At night, our brains can feel full from the day, and our bodies can be buzzing with everything that's happened (even though we might also be quite tired).

Before you go to bed, repeat the mindfulness meditation practice from page 54. (You can even do it in bed, if you are not worried about falling asleep mid-meditation.) When you have finished, answer these questions.

What was the experience like at the end of the day? What did you notice tonight? Before you finish, list three things you are grateful for, large or small:

....

....

....

....

....

....

....

....

....

....

....

Gratitude

Look back at what you did in this section about mindfulness. Take a moment to notice what you are grateful for and write it down here.

DON'T
BELIEVE
EVERYTHING
YOU THINK.

thoughts

From a biological standpoint, thoughts are physical things: electrochemical reactions created when synapses fire between neurons. At any given time, we have billions of neurons talking to each other in our brains—mostly in the background, keeping us safe, happy, and alive.

While scientists understand very little about the nature of consciousness, they do know that thoughts themselves have physical mass; they consist of ions, molecules, and energy exchange. In this way, thoughts are not conceptual—they are, indeed, actual physical things.

Thoughts carry information, report physical sensations, offer up memories, and work in abstractions—they're endlessly complex. Sometimes, thoughts tell us stories about who we are or how to interpret what is going on around us. It's these stories—these "cognitive schemas"—that can contribute to anxiety.

When we live with anxiety, we tend to have what's called an "overactive danger schema," meaning that we are hyper-attuned to threats and negative interpretations. (Remember, this is not about us being negative people who just can't seem to "see the positive"; it's about us having had experiences that taught us that we need to protect ourselves.)

Thoughts are not actually us; they are not our consciousness, awareness, heart, soul, or identity. We are not our thoughts. We are the *observers* of our thoughts. And as the observers, we can examine the patterns they follow, perhaps begin to understand why those patterns were created, and learn to work with and change our thoughts. It's pretty powerful.

Mindfulness is really important in this process, because in order to choose how we react to our thoughts, we need a moment of pause in which to make that conscious choice. If we are used to going from a trigger directly to a reaction, then our first gift to ourselves is to space those things out a bit, to make some room for conscious thought and consideration. We become the conscious observer first, and then we become the conscious decision-maker.

When two people's anxiety seems to react differently to the same scenario, this often has to do with a higher baseline of anxiety. Let's say a few things happen to two people sitting in the same room: maybe there is a weird smell, someone new walks into the room, and there is a loud banging at the door.

Take a look at what might happen to each person:

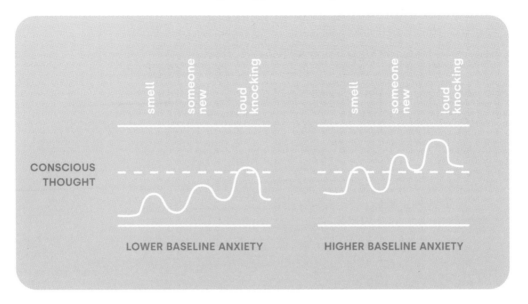

As you can see, the person with the lower baseline doesn't even consciously notice anything amiss until the banging at the door starts; even then, it's a mild anxiety response. The experience for the person with higher baseline anxiety is really different, though. They had several anxious responses building on top of each other, which is that anxiety cycle building.

The good news is that we can bring down our personal anxiety baseline by working with our cognitive schemas—our thought patterns—which is the work we are doing together.

Part of how anxiety tends to reinforce itself is that repeatedly ruminating on something—turning it over in your mind continuously—deepens those specific neural pathways. The more you think about something, the more you think about it, which in itself could be cause for anxiety. Like: "Oh no, I'm having that thought again, I'm going to be stuck here forever!"

Except the observation "I'm having that thought again" is not the thought itself. It is an observation *about* the thought and that means that you are being the observer—the first step to mindfulness. How cool is that? Once you are no longer identifying as the thought, you have begun to do the work of consciously observing your thought patterns. What might feel like worrying about the work is often the beginning of doing the work.

The next step, then, is to consciously offer our brains potential ways to reprogram, restructure, replace, or simply let go of the unhelpful thoughts. One of the key techniques to working with our anxious thoughts is called "cognitive restructuring," which means actively changing our thought patterns. We replace unhelpful fears or untrue thoughts with truths.

This process can sometimes be a little uncomfortable, but the transformative work begins when we can show up for ourselves *within* discomfort. Being able to notice discomfort without running quickly away buys us the ability to choose our responses.

We can work directly with individual thoughts to change them, and we can also root out false and unhelpful "schemas," or frameworks of thinking. These schemas are our kind of macro-level thinking patterns, while an individual thought is on more of a micro level. We want to change both the messaging and the messages, so we will work with both.

And it's okay to admit that life is uncomfortable sometimes! One of the core teachings of Buddhism—one of the Four Noble Truths—is that life is suffering. On the surface, this might seem pessimistic, but there is a power and a wisdom in seeing things as they really are. Still, we can learn to work with suffering, to work with discomfort. (And Buddhism teaches that the path toward both enlightenment and the cessation of suffering is to . . . you guessed it, learn to work with it!)

Let's get to know our thoughts!

My Stories

The most important advocate for you is you—and you don't have to accept anxious thoughts that you don't want to be having. What are some new stories that you want you to hear?

....

....

....

....

....

....

....

....

....

....

....

....

....

....

....

....

....

....

What are some of the thoughts that your anxiety triggers for you?

....
....
....
....
....
....
....
....
....
....
....
....
....
....
....
....
....
....
....
....
....
....
....
....

With these thoughts in mind, what are some of the main overarching stories about you that your anxiety tells you?

....
....
....
....
....
....
....
....
....
....
....
....
....
....
....
....
....
....
....
....
....
....
....

CROSS OFF ANY
OF THESE THAT
NO LONGER SERVE
YOU.

Yes, and . . .

Let's try another way to meet anxious thoughts. This is a strategy used in improv comedy: meeting every idea with "Yes, and . . ."

We'll start by looking at something that truly is difficult for you right now. We'll let that be what it is—sucky—without trying to change it. But we will also notice something that is truly good or even wonderful.

This sucks, it really does: ....
....
....

And while this true, this is actually quite good: ....
....
....

Wonderful! Let's do it some more.

This sucks: ....
....
....

And this is good: ....
....
....

This sucks: ....
....
....

And this is good: ....
....
....

This sucks: ....
....
....

And this is good: ....
....
....

Look at all these true things! Having done this a few times, how does it feel? ....
....
....
....
....
....
....

Flip the Script

Sometimes, it can help to just flip an anxious thought on its head. Let's try that here.

How has your anxiety turned worries into action?

ANXIOUS THOUGHT	FLIPPED SCRIPT
What if he gets mad at me for being late?	*What if we have a great time and feel super connected?*
→	
→	
→	
→	
→	

ANXIOUS THOUGHT	FLIPPED SCRIPT
→	
→	
→	
→	
→	
→	
→	
→	

Mindful Pause

Working with our thoughts is really important work, and it can be very difficult to do. How are you feeling? What are you noticing?

Be the Friend

Let's look at another specific thing in your life that has been making you anxious lately. What is it?

....
....
....
....
....
....
....
....
....
....
....
....
....
....
....
....
....

continues

Imagine what kind of advice a really good and kind friend would give to you about this. Write it down here.

....
....
....
....
....
....
....
....
....
....
....
....
....
....
....
....
....
....
....
....

READ THIS PAGE ALOUD TO YOURSELF IN THE MIRROR. (REALLY, YOU CAN DO IT!)

Gratitude

You are really doing the work it takes to change your anxiety for the long term. This is so awesome! It is not easy, but it matters so much. Take a moment to notice what you feel grateful for right now and write it down here.

ALL FEELINGS OFFER WISDOM.

emotions

Emotions are another phenomenon that is easy to recognize through experience, yet difficult to define.

Neuroscientists, psychologists, and philosophers have no meaningful shared agreement among or between themselves about what emotions are. But we can still work very effectively with them!

We do know that emotions are a combination of cognition (thinking) and bodily perception (physical feelings), plus a bunch of other things we haven't fully understood yet having to do with consciousness, energy fields, and our souls.

Like thoughts, we experience emotions both consciously and unconsciously, and they arise from both conscious and unconscious processes. Our emotional state influences a lot of what happens with our physical bodies: we might experience changes in our memory, attention, or sense perceptions. For instance, if we are feeling scared or threatened, our visual processing becomes enhanced—we actually see more.

And so, emotions both originate from and have influence over the physical body. Emotions aren't separate from our thoughts or bodies. We can't stop feeling any more than we can stop thinking or stop moving; these things make up the whole of the human experience.

As with anxiety, we *learn* our emotional responses. For example, if someone frequently speaks unkindly to us, the sound of their voice—even when they are saying something neutral or even kind—can trigger the same emotional response as when they are saying something unkind.

Developing a relationship with our emotions wherein we trust them, listen to their signals, and work to understand them is crucial for letting our emotions move through us, and for opening up to the deep wisdom that they have to offer us.

When we aren't in direct relationship with our own emotions, they can be weaponized against us—by others and even by ourselves. For instance, if an unkind person says to us, "Why are you acting so emotional? I just asked you to pass the salt!" then we might start to believe that we are overreacting, or "acting crazy." And if we pile on, too: "What is wrong with me? I am freaking out over nothing!" then we've moved far away from the truth of our emotional experience—

which we can trust—and into spinning out about the presence of the emotion themselves.

Additionally, emotions are, in a manner of speaking, contagious. They aren't contagious like a virus, but they are catching in that we parse, internalize, and often reflect the physical expressions of others' emotional states, including facial expressions, vocal affect, and body language such as posture and gestures.

When we do the work to become familiar, and even, yes—friendly!—with our emotions, we're actually looking out for the mental health of not just ourselves, but those around us, too.

We are not our emotions. Emotions, like thoughts, are visitors to us, experiences that we have. They are not our actual identity or self. You are not anger or joy; you are a person *experiencing* anger or joy. Thus, part of our work here is to move away from identifying as an emotion: moving away from "I am happy" toward "I feel happy" or even "happiness is present."

When we identify less *as* emotions and more as a person who *experiences* emotions, we can become more open, more even-keeled, less self-protective, and less reactive. We can become more secure and more grounded. We can experience more calm.

When we explored mindfulness, we looked at how judging what's happening as "bad" or undesirable in some way exacerbates the negative impact of it. The same is true of emotions; when working with emotions, we are often dealing with judgment of the emotions themselves.

This judging of emotions as good or bad, positive or negative, is called *valence.* Valence is a judgment or an appraisal that we associate with an emotional state. It is also sometimes called a positive or negative "charge" of an emotion. And—you probably saw this one coming!—when certain emotions fall under the category of what we've deemed "bad" or wrong, we suffer doubly.

A lot of us have internalized the idea that certain emotions—such as anger or sadness—are bad emotions, or that *we* are somehow bad for having them. (We are not.) A lot of the valence that we apply to emotions has to do with past experience: if we were taught that pride is a bad thing as a child, we tend to experience it as a "bad" emotional state as an adult. We often move from having a strong emotion into having what we believe is a "bad" emotion—from having an experience to having a "bad" experience.

Some scientists now believe that valence is the single biggest factor in how we experience an emotion! Meaning, how good or bad an emotional *feels* depends on how good or bad we believe the emotion *is*. That is pretty wild, eh? And without doing the intentional work to understand our own personal emotional valences, we can move through life not even understanding that different people experience emotions differently—or that we can thoughtfully change our experience of our own emotions.

At the same time that we judge individual emotions, sometimes we judge even the mere presence of emotions. Some of us have been taught to believe that any strong emotion—or any display of emotion at all—is a bad thing. So let me say explicitly: emotions, having emotions, feeling emotions, and processing emotions are *good* things. In much the same way that we learned our anxiety is based on real experiences, so too do our emotions arise from real experiences. Emotions occur because of real events—thoughts, sounds, emotional expressions from other people, memories, interactions, and so on.

And, as with anxiety, we can work to understand—and even befriend—our emotions. Doing so helps us regain our power and develop a deeper relationship with ourselves.

Let's feel into it.

Meeting My Emotions

You are going to take a look at your own personal judgments about emotions, or how "good" or "bad" you perceive them to be. The makeup of our personal valence chart often comes from personal lived experiences. You are not a good or bad person for thinking a certain way about a certain emotion, so try as best as you can to let go of any moral judgments that might come up as you explore this facet of yourself.

Circle roughly 20 to 25 emotions that you can relate to experiencing. If there are any important ones missing for you, add them!

Adoring	Contented	Excited	Loving	Shy
Amused	Craving	Frustrated	Miserable	Stressed
Angry	Curious	Gloomy	Nervous	Surprised
Antsy	Cynical	Grieving	Nostalgic	Tender
Anxious	Delighted	Happy	Offended	Terrified
Ashamed	Depressed	Hopeful	Optimistic	Triumphant
Attracted	Desirous	Impatient	Pessimistic	Trusting
Awed	Disappointed	Infuriated	Playful	Uncomfortable
Bored	Disapproving	Irritable	Proud	Unsatisfied
Calm	Disgusted	Joyful	Relieved	Unsure
Compassionate	Empathetic	Kind	Restless	Worried
Confident	Enthralled	Longing	Sad	....
Confused	Envious	Lost	Satisfied	....

Personal Valence Chart

Using the emotions that you circled on the previous page, plot them here, according to whether you generally think of them as "good" emotions or "bad" ones, and according to how strongly or weakly you generally tend to experience them.

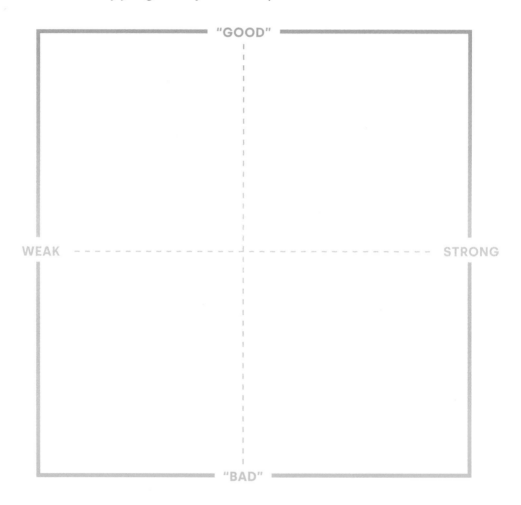

"GOOD"

WEAK — STRONG

"BAD"

Examining My Emotions

Looking at your own personal valence chart, pick three emotions to examine just a little bit more.

EMOTION ....

What thoughts tend to come up for you around this? ....

....

....

What physical sensations tend to come up for you around this?

....

....

What is a common reaction or coping behavior that tends to happen in response to this emotion? ....

....

....

EMOTION ....

What thoughts tend to come up for you around this? ....

....

....

....

What physical sensations tend to come up for you around this?

....

....

What is a common reaction or coping behavior that tends to happen in response to this emotion? ....

....

....

EMOTION ....

What thoughts tend to come up for you around this?

....

....

What physical sensations tend to come up for you around this?

....

....

What is a common reaction or coping behavior that tends to happen in response to this emotion? ....

....

....

....

Mindful Pause

Reviewing our work together so far in working with emotions, do you notice any patterns or surprises? What else do you notice?

Emotions Meditation

Instead of reacting emotionally, it is possible to react as an emotion *ally*—meaning that we can greet, welcome, and seek to understand our emotions without being hijacked by them. We can make friends with our emotions, and they in turn can be our allies, too.

1. Find a relatively quiet, private space, and set a timer (for 5 to 20 minutes, up to you).

2. Stretch out, then settle into a comfortable, upright posture.

3. Gently rest or close your eyes.

4. Take a moment to check in with yourself: How do you feel emotionally? Physically? Energetically?

5. Take a few long, deep breaths, focusing on the exhale.

6. Allow your awareness to expand to fully encompass your emotional experience.

7. When you notice an emotion arising, greet it by name ("Hello, *emotion name*! I notice that you are here.")

8. Allow the emotion to be present, without trying to change it or push it away.

9. When you feel ready, ask the emotion: "Do you have a message you want me to hear today, *emotion name*?"

10. Allow yourself to stay open; there may or may not be a message to be shared.

11. When the emotion is ready to dissipate, thank it by name and tell it that you are ready for it to go.

12. As other emotions arise, greet and interact with them similarly.

13. After the timer, take a final moment to check in with yourself once more. Has anything changed or shifted?

Shorter (5-Minute) Meditation Reflection

In the meditation on page 94, what emotions came up for you?

....

....

....

....

....

....

....

....

....

....

....

....

....

....

....

....

continues

Did your emotional state change over the course of the meditation?

....
....
....
....
....
....
....
....
....
....
....
....
....
....
....
....
....
....
....
....
....
....

PLACE YOUR HAND OVER YOUR HEART AND GIVE YOURSELF A MOMENT OF GRATITUDE FOR DOING THE PRACTICE.

Longer (20-Minute) Meditation Reflection

Which emotions arose for you while doing the meditation on page 94?

....

....

....

....

....

....

....

What was your initial reaction to them?

....

....

....

....

....

....

....

continues

What was different this time around in comparison to the shorter meditation?

....

....

....

....

....

....

....

....

....

Did you notice different emotions come up for you this time around?

....

....

....

....

....

....

....

....

....

PLACE YOUR HAND OVER YOUR HEART AND GIVE YOURSELF A MOMENT OF GRATITUDE FOR DOING THE PRACTICE.

Reflection

Throughout this work, have you felt any moments of release, or any moments of holding or gripping? How do you interpret this?

....

....

....

....

....

....

....

....

....

....

....

....

....

....

....

....

....

....

....

....

What are some keys things that you want to remember from our work on emotions?

....
....
....
....
....
....
....
....
....
....
....
....
....
....
....
....
....
....
....
....
....
....
....

Gratitude

Emotional work can feel really raw, vulnerable, and gratifying. But you did it! I hope that you are able to feel proud of yourself. What are you feeling grateful for, right now in this moment?

THE BODY
NEEDS
SLOWNESS
TO FEEL
SAFE.

body

Anxiety often both originates in and manifests from our physical bodies. Knowing this, we can understand why working with our bodies is one of the most important elements in helping to calm our anxiety.

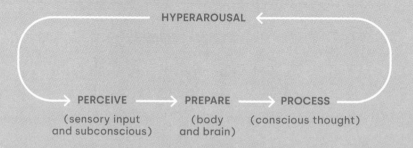

In our bodies, anxiety develops and builds over three stages.

HYPERAROUSAL

PERCEIVE ⟶ PREPARE ⟶ PROCESS

(sensory input
and subconscious)

(body
and brain)

(conscious thought)

This simplified and rewritten model is based on a synthesis presented by psychiatrist Aaron T. Beck and clinical psychologist David A. Clark.

PERCEIVE: As humans, we are constantly, subconsciously scanning our environment, looking for danger that we might need to become consciously aware of. Our unconscious awareness does this ongoing work by reviewing and surfacing sensory inputs like noises, smells, or maybe seeing a person or situation that we don't recognize. This is our automatic threat detection system looking out for us.

PREPARE: Once we unconsciously perceive a potential threat, our body and brain begin to prepare us. Primal things start happening, like our nervous system ramping up, feeling fear or other strong emotions, and potentially starting to feel an aversion. This is where our nervous system gets aroused, or in the case of anxiety, hyperaroused. This is also when we might start to get that "something is not quite right here" feeling, or intuition, kicking in. If we are tuned in, this is when we can start to become aware that alarm bells are going off.

PROCESS: Now—several stages into the cycle already!—is when conscious thought kicks in. If we are predisposed to anxiously interpreting things, then what is likely to happen next is that we start engaging in coping mechanisms. At this point, we may begin to become hyperaroused, and so our threat detection system gets put on high alert. We notice even more potential threats, and the cycle starts repeating. This creates the "loop" of anxiety.

The good news is that we can get out of that loop, because at the point when our nervous system tends to rev up, we can use conscious somatic (body) practices to slow it down instead.

Neurologists categorize our autonomic nervous system response into two parts: sympathetic and parasympathetic. The sympathetic nervous system is the mechanism that moves us into survival mode; it causes our fight, flight, fawn, freeze, or collapse responses. When we are hyperaroused, this is what is triggered.

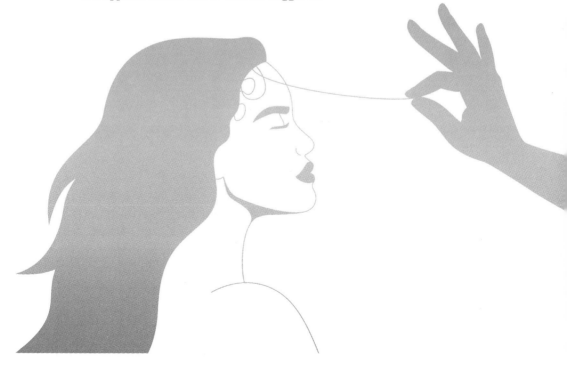

Our parasympathetic nervous system is the part of our autonomic nervous system that induces calm. When we stimulate our parasympathetic nervous system, we move ourselves into what is sometimes called "rest-and-digest" mode—our muscles and organs relax, our breathing slows and deepens, our heart rate goes down, and we shift out of hyperawareness or feeling overstimulated into "chill mode."

A primary component of our parasympathetic nervous system is the vagus nerve, which is the longest nerve in our bodies. The vagus nerve branches from our brains out into a lot of different places in our bodies: our ears, our throat, our neck, our lungs, major organs like our liver, spleen, and kidneys, throughout our torso, and all the way down through our digestive system.

Here's the amazing thing about the vagus nerve: we can use it to talk to our brain. We can actually physically stimulate it to activate our parasympathetic nervous system. Activating our vagus nerve is a little bit like a "calm" button. And it can really work!

Remarkably, 80 percent or more of the messages that the vagus nerve sends actually move from the body to the brain, so in this incredible way, we are able to work with our body to send messages to our brain to calm down. It's so cool!

One of the most powerful ways to stop the cycling of the anxiety loop is to meet the moment of hyperarousal directly with nervous system calming practices. These simple practices are powerful tools that act as a system reset, allowing our agitated bodies to calm down and our threat detection systems to shift out of overdrive.

We develop awareness of what's happening in our bodies through a process called interoception, which means that we become aware of the physical sensations happening inside of our bodies. By learning to mindfully and safely check in with our bodies, we can begin to have more control over our experiences with anxiety.

Let's give some of those practices a try!

Where Does My Anxiety Live?

Thinking about the symptoms of your personal anxiety, where do they live in your body? Draw or write them where they live. (Feel free to embellish the drawing to make it look more like yours before you add your symptoms.)

TAKE A SLOW, DEEP BREATH, AND THEN EXHALE EVEN MORE SLOWLY TO LET GO OF ANYTHING YOU DON'T NEED RIGHT NOW, IN THIS MOMENT.

I ♥ This

You already know many of the ways anxiety can make your body feel uncomfortable. But let's set those aside for a moment and take a look at some of the sense perceptions that you love—things that bring you joy, delight, or feelings of calm.

Sounds I love to hear: ....
....
....
....
....

Things I love to look at: ....
....
....
....
....

Good smells: ....
....
....
....
....
....

Delicious tastes: ....

....

....

....

Touches that feel good: ....

....

....

....

Energy I love to feel: ....

....

....

....

Emotions I enjoy: ....

....

....

....

Looking back over this wonderful list you made, how do
you feel? ....

....

....

....

Vagus Nerve Practices

These are practices that calm our nervous system and give us a chance to get out of the anxiety loop. They bring our nervous system down a notch and give us an opportunity to reset.

Remember, in the same way that anxiety breeds anxiety, calm breeds calm. So, the more you do these—whether you're anxious or not—the more calm you are inviting into your life.

Belly Breathing

Deep, slow belly breathing (aka "diaphragmatic breathing") is the quickest way to send your body the signal that you are okay.

Sitting in a relaxed but upright posture, place one hand on your belly—just above your belly button—and exhale completely. Take a slow, deep inhale into the spot where your hand is—you'll notice your hand rising. Hold that breath a few beats, then exhale slowly, deeply, completely, as your hand falls; pause a few beats after you exhale. Repeat this practice for a few minutes, focusing on making your exhale longer than your inhale. (Try to do this for a full 5 minutes or so the first time you try it.) Go *slowly*.

What was this experience like for you?

Four Spot Tapping

Using two fingers on one hand, gently tap the spot shown on the other hand. If you're not sure of the "right" spot, just move around slowly until it feels right to you. Slowly tap this spot for a full minute, while you breathe slowly, focusing on a deep exhale. After a minute, switch sides, and tap the other hand. (You might notice that you are inclined to tap harder or softer, or faster or slower. Listen to that.)

Next, locate a spot about 3 inches in from your shoulders and about 3 inches down from your collarbone. You will know when you find the spot, because it will be the spot that's sore (it's actually called "the sore spot"). Tap both sides at the same time for a full minute, using whatever pressure and rhythm feels best for you.

What was this experience like for you?

....

....

....

....

....

....

FIND EVEN MORE NERVOUS SYSTEM CALMING PRACTICES AT LIZAKINDRED.COM/ ANXIETY-JOURNAL- EXTRAS

Body Scan Meditation

Body scan meditations are wonderful ways to help us open to and connect with our physical and energetic bodies. You can do a short meditation of 10 minutes or do it for up to 30 minutes.

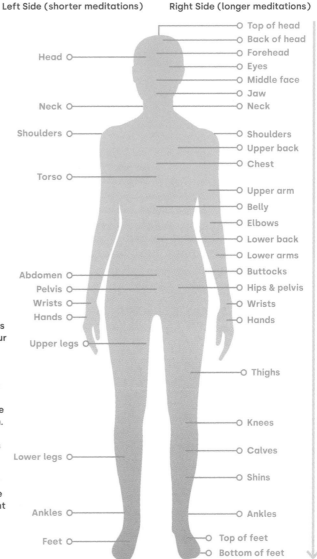

Left Side (shorter meditations)   Right Side (longer meditations)

- Head
- Neck
- Shoulders
- Torso
- Abdomen
- Pelvis
- Wrists
- Hands
- Upper legs
- Lower legs
- Ankles
- Feet

- Top of head
- Back of head
- Forehead
- Eyes
- Middle face
- Jaw
- Neck
- Shoulders
- Upper back
- Chest
- Upper arm
- Belly
- Elbows
- Lower back
- Lower arms
- Buttocks
- Hips & pelvis
- Wrists
- Hands
- Thighs
- Knees
- Calves
- Shins
- Ankles
- Top of feet
- Bottom of feet

If you choose the shorter meditation, move your awareness through the broader areas of your body, as outlined on the left side of the body illustration on this page. For the longer meditation, allow your awareness to be a bit more granular, noticing smaller areas at a time, as outlined on the right side of the body illustration. Move from the top of your body to the bottom, and do both sides together as much as possible— when you are noticing your wrists, for instance, expand your awareness to allow you to notice both your left wrist and your right wrist, together.

1. In a quiet, private space, stretch your body.

2. Settle into a comfortable, supported posture.

3. Gently rest or close your eyes.

4. Take a moment to check in with yourself: How do you feel emotionally? Physically? Energetically?

5. Take a few long, deep breaths, focusing on the exhale.

6. Begin your timer and start the meditation.

7. Bring your focused attention to your breath, noticing where you feel it and what it feels like.

8. Drop the focus on your breath and expand your awareness to include your head.

9. Notice any tension in this area and, as you exhale, let it drain out.

10. After a moment, drop your focus on this area of your body, and expand your awareness to include the next area.

11. Continue to shift your awareness down through the other areas of your body. As your mind wanders, simply bring your attention back.

12. When you reach your feet, pay particular attention to releasing here, especially through the soles of your feet.

13. Take a final moment to check in with yourself once more. Has anything shifted? How do you feel?

14. Move your body in whatever way feels good to come out of the meditation.

Did you find yourself feeling resistant to scanning any particular areas of your body, rushing through certain areas, or wanting to stay in some areas longer? (This is totally normal!) If so, what areas were they?

....
....
....
....
....
....
....
....

Sometimes this resistance matches with our personal "schemas" and stories; does that idea resonate with you? Why or why not?

....
....
....
....
....
....
....
....

IF YOUR TIMER GOES OFF BEFORE YOU ARE THROUGH, GO AHEAD AND FINISH. IT'S A GOOD IDEA TO ALWAYS END FOCUSING ON THE BOTTOM OF YOUR FEET—THIS HELPS TO BOTH CONCLUDE THE MEDITATION AND GROUND YOU.

Mindful Pause

How are you feeling about the work you've done with your body? If you could send one message to your body right now, what would it be?

Progressive Muscle Relaxation

A variation on a body scan meditation is called progressive muscle relaxation (PMR). This meditation is a way to bring awareness to certain areas of the body by working with them physically. It is a great tool for fully releasing anything that is being held there that no longer serves you. You can use the body illustration on page 113 for this practice.

1. In a quiet, private space, stretch your body.

2. Settle into a comfortable, supported posture.

3. Gently rest or close your eyes.

4. Take a moment to check in with yourself: How do you feel emotionally? Physically? Energetically?

5. Take a few long, deep breaths, focusing on the exhale.

6. Begin your timer, and start the meditation.

7. Bring your focused attention to your breath, noticing where you feel it and what it feels like.

8. Drop the focus on your breath and expand your awareness to include your head.

9. TENSE your muscles in this area, holding them tightly but comfortably for a moment (a full breath cycle or two).

10. Then RELEASE and RELAX the area fully, exhaling deeply as you do. Notice how this area feels.

11. Drop your focus on this area of your body, and expand your awareness to include the next area.

12. Repeat the TENSE, RELEASE, and RELAX here.

13. Continue this sequence down through the other areas of your body. End with your feet.

14. Take a final moment to rest fully in your entire body.

15. Check in with yourself once more. Has anything changed or shifted? How do you feel?

16. When you are ready, move your body in whatever way feels good to come out of the meditation.

What was this experience like for you? Were there any particular areas of your body that you noticed a lot of tension in? Were they surprising, or expected? Why?

....

....

....

....

....

....

....

....

....

....

....

....

....

THIS IS A GREAT PRACTICE TO GUIDE YOURSELF THROUGH IF YOU ARE SUFFERING FROM INSOMNIA.

What Can I Do for You Today, Body?

We've spent some time paying close attention to our own bodies and our needs. Now that we know our personal anxiety symptoms and a little bit more about where we tend to hold our physical tension, let's take that information and turn it into things we can do for ourselves. What is one specific, concrete, relatively easy thing that you can do for your body, in each of these categories? And when will you do it? Come back and mark it off when it is done.

	FOOD	SLEEP	TECHNOLOGY
What			
When			
	DONE	DONE	DONE

	NATURE	MOVEMENT	CALM
What			
When			
	DONE	DONE	DONE

Gratitude

Although it might not behave or look exactly as you wish it would, your body is always working hard for you. Our bodies may be imperfect, but they are trying their best! And while they might send mixed messages at times, they are also full of so much wisdom. What are you feeling grateful for about your body, and the work you've done with it here?

DIRECT
EXPERIENCE
IS THE
ONLY
CONFIRMATION.

experience

One of the hallmarks of anxiety is that when we experience it, we adapt to it by minimizing our exposure to the things that cause it. To avoid anxiety, we avoid the things that make us feel anxious. As a self-protection mechanism, this makes sense. You don't like X, so you don't do it. I don't like onions, so I don't eat them—problem solved. I don't need to eat more onions to know I don't like them. (Sorry, onions.)

The trouble is, we're so good at learning to avoid the things that make us anxious that our smart and helpful brains, which are truly concerned with our survival, are like, "Cool! She doesn't want onions! I shall scan the environment vigorously for onions and send out high alert messages whenever I suspect that onions are nearby!"

And suddenly the whole world smells suspiciously like onions—except "onions" are people giving me potentially weird looks and my brain is exploding with alerts that nearly everyone I come across is very possibly giving me a weird look and what did I ever do to them anyway?

exhale

Okay. So. This is why one of the things we do to work with our anxiety is to recalibrate the danger signals around the things that are stressing us out—to have some new experiences that our brains can file away under "this is fine." It isn't about pretending things are okay when they are not—we're not lying to ourselves. This is about gathering data about the way the world actually is, letting the things that are *actually* fine be categorized as such.

But as we learned earlier, our thinking brain is kind of the last person to show up at the anxiety party. So, to communicate with the earlier arrivals—sense perception, threat analysis, physical arousal, all the primal brain partygoers—our work here is to intentionally go out and have some new experiences. Doing this can allow us to recalibrate the danger signals on these things and let these party people take it down a notch.

The reason we work with the *very things* that are stressing us out isn't because we need more stress in our lives—it's because these are the things that are stressing us out, and thus causing anxiety. In order to reduce the anxiety that certain things bring into our lives, we have to work *with* them.

As we go through the process of having some new experiences, it's important to know that you are in charge. Yes, you are going to lean

into some things that might make you uncomfortable, but you are also going to lean away from them, too—and you'll be in control.

This process of leaning in and leaning out is called pendulation.

Think of it similarly to how we might ease into a hot bath. Much like a pendulum, we dip our toes in—experience it a little—and then back out. Then, once we know it's uncomfortable but safe, we go in a little bit deeper. We go through the process of "lean in / back off / process / repeat" until we are fully immersed and adjusting well.

This process is sometimes also called "looping" because, as you can see, we are moving through a state of arousal and a state of calm, over and over.

As we work directly but gently with our anxiety—as we loop or pendulate slowly through these experiences—what we are gradually doing is increasing what is called our "window of tolerance," which is the level of experience in which we feel safe. (This phrase was originally coined by Dr. Dan Siegel.)

When we feel threatened, we go into a survival mode: fight, flight, freeze, fawn, or collapse. What we want to do is to gently increase, or widen, our window of tolerance—so that we can comfortably have a bigger variety of experiences before our anxiety grabs control.

We do this by gently leaning on the edges of our experiences, using pendulation to keep us safe and in control.

What we are doing is recalibrating our "attentional bias to threat" to similar levels that non-anxious people have. To become immune to threat detection would cause its own problems; we would no longer be able to keep ourselves safe. However, we will benefit from experiencing the world a little more like a non-anxious person does. We aren't using an on/off switch; we are using a dimmer switch—or, widening the window.

We do this work by practicing somatic awareness, which is, simply, the practice of being aware of our soma (our body, taken from the Greek). Somatic awareness is like mindfulness for the body—observing from the messages our body is sending us and choosing what to do with the information.

As we do this work together, remember: we know how to work with discomfort, and we know that this is where transformative change happens. We have the tools and strategies to do this work: mindfulness, pendulation, and love for ourselves.

So with you in charge, let's look at how you can gradually work to open your windows and let some more fresh air in!

Ice Cube Meditation

This short practice gives us some insight into how we experience discomfort. Approach this with a spirit of curiosity, of getting some insight into your typical reactions. If you need to take a break, it's okay to set the ice cube down and pick it back up, but do your best to sit with the discomfort as much as possible—this is where the insight happens.

1. Place an ice cube in a bowl in front of you and settle into a comfortable supported meditation posture.

2. Take a few deep, slow breaths.

3. When you are ready, pick up the ice cube in your hand.

4. Notice how it feels physically: stinging, tingling, burning, etc.

5. As you continue to hold the ice cube, notice your thoughts.

6. Notice how you feel emotionally.

7. Let the feeling become more intense as you continue to notice all of your reactions: physical, emotional, and thoughts.

8. Do you notice aversions? Rushing? Powering through?

9. As you continue to hold the ice cube and experience discomfort, notice whether your reactions change. Sit with it.

10. Set the ice cube back in the bowl.

11. Notice how that feels—physically, emotionally, and cognitively. Really sit with the changes.

12. Take a few more deep breaths and come out of the practice.

How did you feel in the midst of the discomfort?

....

....

....

....

....

....

....

....

....

How did you feel after you set it down?

....

....

....

....

....

....

....

....

....

....

....

....

THIS PRACTICE IS SUPPOSED TO BRING US INTO CONVERSATION WITH DISCOMFORT, SAFELY. IF YOU HAVE A PHYSICAL CONDITION THAT CONTRAINDICATES HOLDING AN ICE CUBE, SUBSTITUTE ANOTHER PHYSICAL SENSATION THAT IS SAFE BUT UNCOMFORTABLE.

What did you learn about your reactions to discomfort from
this practice?

....
....
....
....
....
....
....
....
....

How might what you learned about how you respond to discomfort
translate into other parts of your life?

....
....
....
....
....
....
....
....
....
....
....
....

Windows I Have Shut

Let's look at some of the things that you tend to avoid due to anxiety. They may be things that have a large impact (like never driving, or rarely speaking up in group settings) or a small impact (like never leaving home without an extra phone charger). What do you avoid due to anxiety? Fill in the windows.

WHEN YOU ARE FINISHED, TAKE ANOTHER QUIET MOMENT TO THANK YOUR ANXIETY FOR LETTING YOU LOOK AT IT CLEARLY.

Mindful Pause

You just examined how you deal with discomfort and looked at some of the windows that your anxiety has caused you to shut. How did that make you feel, and what do you want to remember from this?

From Avoiding to Allowing

Read back through your closed windows (page 130) and consider which ones you might feel ready to work with and explore a little bit. Pick three, and list them in the left column below. Once you've listed them, write a bit about how they have allowed you to have short-term safety, how they have helped you manage in the moment. (Know that what you've done has been helpful, but it's okay to move on.) Write a long-term lesson you might be able to teach your anxiety by opening the window back up a little wider. How might widening this window be helpful to you in the long run?

MY WINDOW	SHORT-TERM SAFETY	LONG-TERM LESSON
Example: Go somewhere out of cell phone service	*Helps me feel connected and safe*	*Opens me to new experiences and teaches me that I can adapt in caring for myself*

MY WINDOW	SHORT-TERM SAFETY	LONG-TERM LESSON

CLOSE WITH GRATITUDE.

Widen the Windows

It's time to widen the windows a little. Eventually, we will do this by taking small steps, using pendulation (leaning in and out) to keep us safe—but for now, we're just imagining what small steps we might take to get us to a big step.

What is one window you listed on the previous page?

....

....

....

....

....

....

....

What small steps could you take that would allow you to widen that window up to a point where it is no longer controlling your behavior?

....

....

....

....

....

....

Choose another window you listed on the previous page.

....
....
....
....
....
....
....
....
....

What small steps could you take that would allow you to widen that window up to a point where it is no longer controlling your behavior?

....
....
....
....
....
....
....
....

Exposure and Experience Experiments

You are going to take some steps to reexperience some of the things you have been avoiding, by moving off the page and into the laboratory of your own life. By doing this, you will begin to increase how much you can comfortably tolerate. Here's how to do these experiments in a way that gives you long-term benefits and still feels relatively safe while you do them:

+ Invite mindfulness along as a partner while you do these experiments.

+ You will feel some discomfort. But at the point of that discomfort, if you are able to lean in just a tiny bit more before you lean back out, then you are doing the work to move toward more long-term calm.

+ Remember that you might become hyper- or hypoaroused; as you take these steps, simply notice whether you start becoming worked up or begin to zone out. Anything that starts feeling "extra" is the edge of your window of tolerance—this is the place to lean in just a tad, and then lean back out a bit, until you feel safe enough to continue. Remember, it's a slow process.

+ Find your own flow in the pendulation as you take the small steps that you already outlined. Forward and back—it's kind of like a dance. We are not throwing ourselves out of our safety zones; we are dancing at the edges—and you are always in charge.

Experiment #1

Write down which window you're working on at the moment, then create three steps that you are taking to help you widen your window of tolerance. Fill in the categories under each step. What are your worries before you do the step? What do you feel or think are some likely scenarios to come out of this step? What is the actual outcome after completing this step?

What window are you working on? ....

STEP 1: TAKE THE STEP		
WORRIES BEFORE	LIKELY SCENARIO	ACTUAL OUTCOME

STEP 2: TAKE THE STEP		
WORRIES BEFORE	LIKELY SCENARIO	ACTUAL OUTCOME

STEP 3: TAKE THE STEP		
WORRIES BEFORE	LIKELY SCENARIO	ACTUAL OUTCOME

Experiment #2

What window are you working on? ....

STEP 1: TAKE THE STEP		
WORRIES BEFORE	LIKELY SCENARIO	ACTUAL OUTCOME

STEP 2: TAKE THE STEP		
WORRIES BEFORE	LIKELY SCENARIO	ACTUAL OUTCOME

STEP 3: TAKE THE STEP		
WORRIES BEFORE	LIKELY SCENARIO	ACTUAL OUTCOME

Reflection

What have you learned from these experiments?

....
....
....
....
....
....
....
....
....
....
....
....
....
....
....
....
....
....
....
....
....
....

Which window would you like to focus on opening even further? How can you do this?

....
....
....
....
....
....
....
....
....
....
....
....
....
....
....
....
....
....
....
....
....
....

Gratitude

You are amazing! Take a look back at what you did in this section about experiencing. Take a moment to notice what you are grateful for and write it down here.

I AM

COMPLETE.

JUST NOT

FINISHED.

forward from here

Throughout this journal, we have explored, examined, and experienced myriad facets of our anxiety. As we know, anxiety doesn't get "cured"—because it's actually a self-protection mechanism that we need to survive—but we also know that we can completely shift our way of relating to our anxiety and we can learn to have it work for us, instead of being ruled by it.

Calming our anxiety is very much an ongoing process. By now, you know a lot more about your own anxiety: what it is trying to tell you, the ways in which it has become misguided, some of the places it stems from, and your own most personally effective ways to calm your anxiety. Maybe you've even learned to love or appreciate your anxiety a little bit.

In order to keep moving along your journey with anxiety, it's important that you continue to implement the skills and strategies you've learned here. (You are always welcome to revisit any of the practices in the book—or start over again from the beginning. It's an ongoing journey that builds and grows.)

For some people, it can be helpful to move forward by thinking about anxiety like a loving but sometimes overbearing parent or caregiver—someone who loves you (and whom you love) but tends to overreact sometimes. We can love that person and appreciate what they are trying to do for us without letting them control our life. That is what anxiety is: a helpful thing that actually *does* have our best interests in mind, but sometimes acts in ways that are unhelpful.

We've looked a lot at how and why anxiety tends to spiral—and how and why we interrupt it determines whether we are working *with* it or reinforcing the damaging effects. Our goal is to keep our worries healthy and helpful and not let anxiety take over, but to serve us instead.

The final step on our path—setting goals for what's next—is an important one to take, in order to complete the transition into a life of more calm. Along our journey together, we've learned a lot of ways to proactively deal with anxiety in its different manifestations and figured out how to stop the anxiety from spinning out into a self-reinforcing cycle. And this is so wonderful!

But our aim is even higher: to intentionally and consciously transform our lives. To do this, we are going to set some goals— specific, personal goals, ranging from small steps to big dreams. And we are going to come back and mark down when we've reached these goals, because this is a new cycle we are stepping into and we want to reinforce it.

As you move through these goals, know that you can set them all at once, and come back as you meet them, or do one and then another, sequentially. However you do this is fine—just as long as you keep doing it.

I am so proud of the work we've done together here! I hope you are, too.

Let's move forward.

Best-Case Scenario

As you continue to work with your anxiety, what is the best-case outcome in your life?

....
....
....
....
....
....
....
....

What will be different in my life as that outcome unfolds?

....
....
....
....
....
....
....
....
....
....

Try This, Not That

How can you shift your everyday coping mechanisms from things that bring short-term relief from anxiety to things that offer longer-term calm?

....
....
....
....
....
....
....
....
....
....
....
....
....
....
....
....
....
....
....

My Quick and Easy Anxiety Goal

Goals help us move forward and build trust in ourselves. Let's set a quick and easy goal for something that will help you move toward more calm in your life. Make it a SMART goal—specific, measurable, achievable, relevant, and time-bound (has a deadline!).

In the next few days, what will you do?

....

....

....

....

....

....

Once you've accomplished the goal, come back and check in.

How did achieving this goal make you feel?

....

....

....

....

....

My Medium Anxiety Goal

Let's also look at something that you can accomplish in the next few weeks. Remember to keep it SMART—specific, measurable, achievable, relevant, and time-bound (has a deadline!).

In the next few weeks, what will you do?

....

....

....

....

....

....

Once you've accomplished the goal, come back and check in.

How did achieving this goal make you feel?

....

....

....

....

....

....

Mindful Pause

What wisdom have you discovered through leaning into some new experiences and sticking around through discomfort? What has been the most eye-opening thing for you, and what do you want to remember as you continue to work on more goals?

My Big Ol' Anxiety Goal

Now let's take a look at something that you can accomplish in the next few months. It can be something big, that you might be a bit intimidated to start but that you know will make a big difference. This goal should also be SMART: specific, measurable, achievable, relevant, and time-bound (has a deadline).

In the next few months, what will you do?

....
....
....
....
....
....

Once you've accomplished the goal, come back and check in.

How did achieving this goal make you feel?

....
....
....
....
....
....

Dream Big Backward

Declare a big goal! Then write out the steps it will take, working backward. (For instance, if your goal is to travel internationally, working backward you might need to open a savings account, fill out a passport application, pick a specific location, start collecting ideas, buy a plane ticket, and book hotels.)

big dream

SECRET TIP: THESE ARE GREAT STEPS TO TAKE WHEN YOU FEEL LIKE PROCRASTINATING ABOUT SOMETHING ELSE. ☺

What I'm Doing Next

With this big dream in mind, write five specific things you are going to do in the next week or so, then check them off when done.

1. ....
   ....
   .... ☐

2. ....
   ....
   .... ☐

3. ....
   ....
   .... ☐

4. ....
   ....
   .... ☐

5. ....
   ....
   .... ☐

Gratitude

You are such an amazing human! Write a love letter to yourself, letting you know how grateful you are for your work, openness, and progress on your anxiety.

Dear .... ,

YOU
HAVE DONE
SUCH DIFFICULT AND
BEAUTIFUL WORK! ON
THE OTHER SIDE OF THIS
PAGE IS YOUR CERTIFICATE OF
COMPLETION. YOU DESERVE IT, I
PROMISE. FILL IN YOUR NAME,
CUT IT OUT, AND ENJOY! YOU
ARE NOT PERFECT, BUT
YOU ARE COMPLETE.

♥

CERTIFICATE OF COMPLETION

of the *Calm Your Anxiety Journal* Presented to

....

Name

This is to certify imperfect but openhearted completion of the
Calm Your Anxiety Journal, and to record for all time that the
above-named human has a beautiful soul, has inherent worth, and
possesses a huge heart and deep inner wisdom.

Date ....

Valid: *Forever*

Liza

Liza Kindred

Further Resources

When you're ready for more, I offer myriad resources about anxiety, meditation, and the self-love journey. You can even take a free, online refresher class on working with anxiety, and I have compiled some resources to get you started finding a qualified therapist. Find all of this at lizakindred.com/anxiety-journal-extras.

My other book, *Eff This! Meditation: 108 Tips, Tricks, and Ideas for When You're Anxious, Stressed Out, or Overwhelmed*, is full of easy, hands-on practices. Many take 5 minutes or less! It's available everywhere books are sold, and is a great complement to this journal.

Want to connect with me? I send out a popular newsletter every Friday with five quick things in it: stuff like free meditation resources, book recommendations, must-see shows, and cool stuff from Mother Nature. I also post short, helpful tips and practices on social media.

Get my Friday love notes :: lizakindred.com/newsletter

 Instagram :: @Liza_K @effthismeditation

 Twitter :: @LizaK @effthismeditate

 See you on the internet!

xo,

Further Reading

Books about Anxiety

The Cambridge Handbook of Anxiety and Related Disorders edited by Bunmi O. Olatunji (750+ pages; very academic, but very interesting)

Embracing Anxiety: How to Access the Genius of This Vital Emotion by Karla McLaren

Mindful Somatic Awareness for Anxiety Release: A Body-Based Approach to Moving Beyond Fear and Worry by Michele L. Blume

Take Back Your Mind: Buddhist Advice for Anxious Times by Lodro Rinzler

The Wisdom of Anxiety: How Worry & Intrusive Thoughts Are Gifts to Help You Heal by Sheryl Paul

Books about Self-Reflection

Belonging Here: A Guide for the Spiritually Sensitive Person by Judith Blackstone

The Body Keeps the Score by Bessel van der Kolk (about trauma)

Self-Compassion: The Proven Power of Being Kind to Yourself by Kristin Neff

Books for When Things Are Awful

It's OK That You're Not OK: Meeting Grief and Loss in a Culture That Doesn't Understand by Megan Devine (Megan's website at RefugeInGrief.com offers wonderful help for humans who are deeply grieving, and people trying to support those who are.)

When Things Falls Apart by Pema Chödrön